O9-ABI-922

ELIZABETH RING

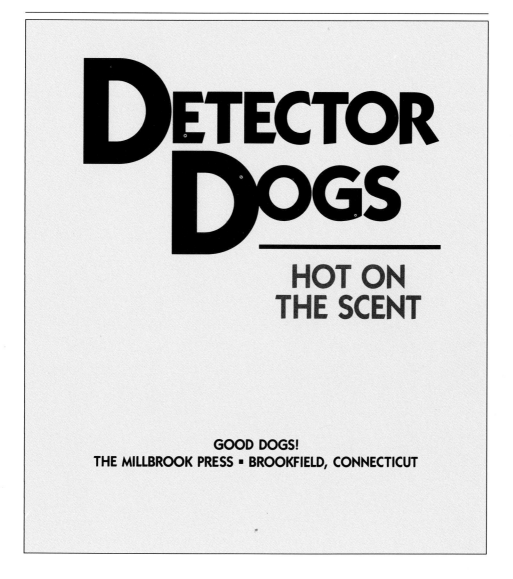

DETECTOR DOGS

HOT ON
THE SCENT

GOOD DOGS!
THE MILLBROOK PRESS ▪ BROOKFIELD, CONNECTICUT

FOR NICK,
MASTER DETECTIVE

Cover photograph courtesy of Ginger Giles

Photographs courtesy of U.S. Department of Agriculture:
pp. 3, 26; Bill Hennefrund: pp. 4, 7, 12, 14, 17, 18;
Reuters/Bettmann: pp. 10, 19; UPI/Bettmann: p. 21;
U.S. Customs Service: p. 23; Photo Researchers: p. 28.

Library of Congress Cataloging-in-Publication Data

Ring, Elizabeth, 1920-
Detector dogs : hot on the scent / by Elizabeth Ring.
p.   cm. — (Good dogs!)
Includes bibliographical references (p.   ) and index.
Summary: Examines the many ways dogs use their keen sense of smell
to help law enforcement personnel in all kinds of detective work.
ISBN 1-56294-289-1 (lib. bdg.)
1. Police dogs—Juvenile literature. 2. Police dogs—Training—
Juvenile literature. [1. Police dogs. 2. Dogs.] I. Title.
II. Series.
HV8025.R53 1993
363.2'32--dc20   93-7275 CIP AC

Published by The Millbrook Press
2 Old New Milford Road
Brookfield, Connecticut 06804

DETECTOR DOGS

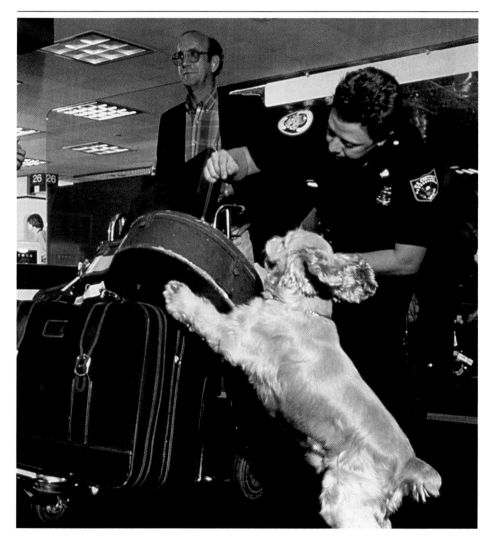

When Yölin, a narcotics-detecting dog, searches a car,
her nose goes over every inch of space.

One spring afternoon, Trooper Michael Wynn and Yölin, a narcotics-detector dog, raced down a Connecticut highway, lights flashing, siren wailing.

Trooper Wynn had just received a call from two police officers who had stopped a speeding car. The officers had found some narcotics in the car and they suspected more were hidden. They needed Yölin's drug-detecting nose.

Yölin, an 80-pound (36-kilogram) German shepherd, lay half asleep on the backseat of Trooper Wynn's car. But the minute Trooper Wynn pulled up behind the stopped car and snapped a leash on Yölin's collar, the dog was wide awake—ears perked, eyes alert, tail wagging, body tense. Sniffing out hidden narcotics was a game the well-trained dog loved to play.

With everyone out of the suspects' car, Trooper Wynn opened the front door on the passenger side. "Seek!" he commanded Yölin.

The dog jumped into the car. She sniffed along the seats and underneath the dashboard. Suddenly, she "hit." That is, her nose told her she had found one of the narcotics she was trained to look for. She immediately sat down, staring hard at the spot. Trooper Wynn checked. Sure enough. Some bags of marijuana were stuffed under the dashboard.

"Good girl, Yölin," Trooper Wynn said. He gave her a pat.

Yölin wagged her tail and went on sniffing—in door pockets, along armrests, in the ashtray, over the sun visors, across the ceiling. Then Trooper Wynn led the dog outside and Yölin sniffed along the car's fenders and bumpers, around the hood and the trunk.

That afternoon, Yölin uncovered thirty packets of marijuana—even one hidden underneath the car, near the muffler. The officers made an arrest, and Yölin got her reward: a tennis ball.

A DOG'S SENSE OF SMELL · A dog's nose is amazing. It can sniff things you and I could never detect. A dog can pick up smells that are in the air, on the ground, underground, underwater, and inside all sorts of coverings.

As in Yölin's case, nothing makes most dogs happier than following a scent. Anyone who has gone for a walk with a sniffing dog knows this. The dog's nose never stops twitching, snuffling, or snorting as it picks up the smell of a chipmunk in a stone wall, a snake down a hole, another dog, a dead squirrel on the road, or anything at the town dump.

A dog's snout is full of sensitive scent cells (also called olfactory or ethmoidal cells). You and I have about five million scent cells, covering an area about the size of a postage stamp, far back up our noses. Dogs have about 200 million scent cells spread over the numerous folds in the linings of their snouts. A dog's sense of smell is a million or more times better than ours. Even flat-faced, small-nosed dogs such as bulldogs and pugs are far better scent detectors than we are. A dog, for instance, can smell one drop of blood in 5 quarts (almost 5 liters) of water or a leak in a gas pipe several feet underground. A good sniffer can

Dogs like Rocky, a German shepherd, use their keen noses to help police and other officials in many kinds of detective work.

detect smells that even sensitive scientific instruments cannot pick up.

Dogs sniff in the same way people do, by taking in a quick breath through their nostrils. Sniffing sharpens a smell, making it easier (for both us and dogs) to identify a particular odor. Unlike our noses (most of the time), the end of a dog's nose is always a bit wet. This moistness helps a dog hold onto smells long enough to memorize them.

While our noses can identify about four thousand different odors, we cannot always separate smells that are closely alike. We have no trouble, for instance, telling the difference between the aromas of popcorn and bacon. But a raw pork chop and a raw lamb chop might smell much the same to us. A dog's nose, however, can easily separate such similar smells.

Largely because of their scenting ability, many dogs are wonderful patrollers, trackers, rescuers, and detectors—which makes dogs of great help to people.

Patrol dogs' noses, for example, help the police track lost people or fleeing criminals. Search-and-rescue dogs follow the scent of lost persons.

This book is about detector dogs (sometimes called "D-dogs"). At police K-9 training centers ("K-9" being short for "canine"—which refers to the dog family), dogs are trained for four kinds of detective work. Each dog is a specialist in one kind of work:

Narcotics-detecting dogs search for illegal drugs, such as marijuana, hashish, heroin, and cocaine.

Bomb-detecting dogs search for explosives, such as dynamite.

Accelerant-detecting dogs search through burned areas for fire-starting substances, such as gasoline and kerosene.

Body-detecting dogs search for people buried in rubble caused by earthquakes, floods, and other disasters.

Police departments are not the only agencies that use detector dogs. The U.S. Customs Service also uses narcotics dogs to search for illegal drugs coming into the United States.

The U.S. Department of Agriculture (USDA) uses other detector-dog specialists to search for illegal food, plants, and animals that are brought into the country.

Some private companies use detector dogs to search for gas leaks, termites, and other things that they need to find in their lines of business.

WHAT MAKES A DETECTOR DOG? · Not all dogs make good detectives. What, besides her wonderful sniffer, makes Yölin so good at what she does? When Yölin was offered as a detector dog to the Connecticut State Police K-9 Training Center in Meriden, Connecticut, Sergeant David Barger went to visit her at her home. As soon as he saw how quickly, accurately, and excitedly Yölin located a ball hidden in a woodpile, he knew that she was a natural for detector work.

Like all dogs chosen to be detectors, Yölin was intelligent, alert, agile, healthy, friendly, faithful, courageous, easy to train, and eager to play the game of "hide and seek!" She also liked to

Detector
dogs work
in many
settings.
Here, a
dog checks
a car for
hidden
explosives
outside
the U.S.
Capitol in
Washington,
D.C.

ride in cars, which is necessary in K-9 service, since police officers are apt to spend a lot of time on the road.

The majority of police-department detector dogs are, like Yölin, German shepherds, but golden retrievers, Labrador retrievers, bloodhounds, and other breeds are used, too. Some dogs are bought from kennels. Some come from animal shelters. Others are donated to police K-9 units by people who, for one reason or another, cannot keep their dogs.

Each dog is examined by a veterinarian to check its health. Each person who donates a dog to the K-9 Training Center fills out a questionnaire, giving details about the dog's temperament, habits, and skills. Such screening means that most dogs that are chosen complete their detector training successfully. Biters and snarlers are never invited to the training "games."

DETECTOR-DOG TRAINING · Detector-dog training educates a dog's natural ability to pick up scents. An untrained dog will follow any smell that interests it. A trained dog (when at work) concentrates on a few smells and knows that locating the source of a particular scent means a reward—a treat, a toy, a game of fetch, or a pat on the head from its partner.

Detector dogs like Yölin specialize in work not expected of most patrol dogs. At most police dog-training schools throughout the country, patrol dogs go through several weeks of a basic course that teaches them the skills they will need in everyday police work. These activities include patrolling roads, protecting people, tracking people, searching buildings, and controlling crowds.

In basic patrol-dog training, dogs not only learn basic obedience (to "sit," "come," "stay," and the like) but go through tough exercises such as jumping through windows on command, climbing ladders, and crawling through pipes.

A game of catch is all the reward narcotics dog Yölin needs for her work. She can catch and hold up to three balls in her mouth at once.

A few patrol dogs may go on to detector-dog training, which takes another eight weeks. Most detector dogs, however, skip the basic course and are taught only how to hunt for particular substances: narcotics, explosives, accelerants, or bodies.

DOGS THAT SEARCH FOR NARCOTICS · During training, a narcotics dog is introduced to the smell of one drug at a time. At first the drug is placed out in the open on the ground. Every time the dog locates the drug, the dog is rewarded with a treat, praise, and pats. Then the drug is hidden, perhaps in a hole in a concrete building block placed among several empty blocks. When the dog sniffs out the drug, it is again rewarded.

The dog quickly gets the idea. It is taught not to pounce on its find—as it might when chasing a ball. Instead, it learns to "alert" (call the trainer's attention) to the drug, by sitting, lying down, barking, or simply standing and looking at the place where the drug is located. As the drug is hidden in ever harder-to-find places, the dog seems to enjoy the challenge—much the way many dogs enjoy leaping higher and higher to catch a Frisbee. Hide-and-seek is a detector dog's favorite game.

As soon as the dog learns to alert regularly to the scent of one drug (perhaps marijuana), dog and trainer start working together with another drug smell (such as hashish), then another (heroin or cocaine). This game practice goes on until the dog can, without fail, zero in on all the odors it is being trained to look for. After that, the games are repeated now and then to keep the scents fresh in the dog's mind.

**A trainer presses on the rump of a black Labrador retriever
to teach the dog to sit when it sniffs a specific odor.**

Sometimes drug smugglers hide narcotics in strong-smelling materials (such as mothballs, onions, gasoline, incense, and even baby powder) to try to fool drug-sniffing dogs. But all dogs have an amazing ability to screen out smells they are *not* searching for, and narcotics dogs are trained to ignore a drug's cover-up.

Detector dogs learn fairly quickly to identify narcotics and to screen out other smells. But it may take a few months to train them to ignore cats, friendly pats from strangers, and other things that can easily take a dog's mind off its business. A well-trained detector dog is so intent on its search that it cannot be distracted by *any*thing.

Trooper Wynn himself trained Yölin, and during their days together, the man and dog "bonded." That is, they formed a real team. Bonding is an important part of a detector dog's training. Yölin spent much of her time with Trooper Wynn—both at work at the training center and at home, at rest and at play. They learned to trust and care for each other—much as you do with a best friend. To Trooper Wynn, Yölin was a loyal partner he could depend on on the job. To Yölin, Trooper Wynn became "father," "master," "boss"—the one she willingly obeyed with a wagging tail.

Being "underdog" in the team came naturally to Yölin. It is in a dog's nature to find its special place in its group—canine or human. Among packs of dogs or wolves (the most probable ancestors of dogs), one animal is accepted by the others as "leader of the pack"—always a superior, dominant animal. Just so, Yölin accepted Trooper Wynn as "top dog," the one who not only gave commands but who also fed and protected her.

DOGS THAT SEARCH FOR EXPLOSIVES · Bomb-detecting dogs are trained in about the same way that narcotics dogs are. Bomb dogs simply repeat the "hide-and-seek" game (with bombs instead of narcotics) until the dogs can find an explosive—fast. In a bomb search, speed is essential, of course (the danger of an explosion always a threat), and a well-trained dog can locate an explosive about twenty times faster than a person can. One dog covered a 50-foot-long (15-meter) hallway in two minutes flat, pinpointing a locker where a bomb was hidden.

A bomb dog learns to recognize and alert to explosives such as dynamite, TNT, and bombs made with certain kinds of black powder or plastics. When the dog discovers one of these, it quietly sits down and "points" with its nose toward the danger spot. Fortunately, bomb dogs are about 95 percent accurate in locating bombs—before they explode.

As with narcotics dogs, bomb dogs are not easily fooled by strong, disguising smells, not even black pepper—which may, however, make a dog sneeze.

For bomb-detector work, many police officers favor golden or Labrador retrievers over other breeds. Retrievers have been found to be calmer, gentler, and lighter on their feet than German shepherds and other large dogs used in police work. Also, retrievers really like to work in water—where they must sometimes search for explosives.

Bomb dogs in military service perform in much the same way as dogs in police work. They are trained by the military forces to detect booby traps, sea mines, and ammunition. Military explosives-detecting dogs must, perhaps, have even calmer dispositions than police bomb-detector dogs. It takes months of training to get them used to such warlike conditions as the noise

Liza, a yellow Labrador retriever, learns to identify the smell of explosives. Each time the spoked wheel spins, the dog sniffs each can to find the one that has the right scent.

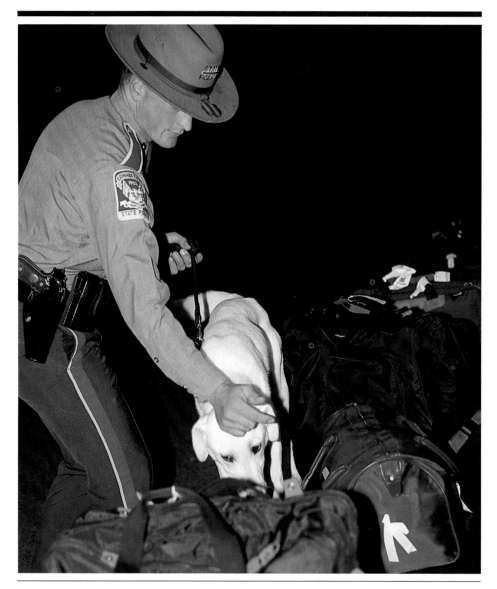

At work at an airport, Liza sniffs luggage before it is put on a plane. She is searching for any explosive material.

Anna, an Air Force bomb-detecting dog, checks a plane for hidden explosives during the 1991 Persian Gulf war.

of firearms and the fury of flames. Many dogs won awards for their work in World War II, during which thousands of dogs were employed as detector dogs, guard dogs, or search-and-rescue dogs.

DOGS THAT SEARCH FOR ACCELERANTS · Sometimes arson (unlawful fire setting) is suspected as the cause of a fire. After such a fire is out and the area cooled off, accelerant-detector dogs are put to work. Sometimes the dogs wear "shoes" on their paws, to protect them from broken glass and other sharp objects hidden in the ashes and rubble. The dogs sniff all around the burned places, searching for the smell of gasoline, kerosene, paint remover, lacquer thinner, or some other accelerant (fire starter).

While accelerants can often be detected by instruments, the instruments sometimes give false information. Trained accelerant dogs are more accurate. They can detect a tiny drop of some fire starter in the debris of a burned-out building. Some dogs can even detect the faintest whiff of an accelerant in material that has been washed or in places that have been scrubbed clean. A good sniffer can locate a fire starter in about half the time it takes a person.

Accelerant-detector dogs include German shepherds, Labrador retrievers, bloodhounds, springer spaniels, and beagles. Some dogs are trained to detect as many as thirty different kinds of fire starters.

DOGS THAT SEARCH FOR BODIES · After a disaster such as a fire, earthquake, flood, the collapse of a building, or in cases when a murder is suspected, body-detector dogs are often called upon to help police investigations.

In police K-9 training, dogs (usually German shepherds)

After a severe earthquake struck San Francisco, California, in 1989, body-detecting dogs helped search the rubble of collapsed buildings.

become familiar with the scent of a dead body. The dogs are introduced not to the smell of actual dead bodies but to chemicals that smell like corpses.

The training process for a body-detector dog is much the same as that for other detector dogs. The dog first sniffs the chemical "corpse" smell, then searches for the scent hidden under rocks, in crevices, behind walls, and other places the dog may have to search when it is on the job. The dog is trained to dig, bark, or sit and point when it locates the smell.

The dog also learns to detect corpse odor in water. From the bow of a boat, the dog sniffs along the surface of the water until it catches the underwater scent. Then it alerts its partner—and gets its reward.

Body-detecting work may seem gruesome to people, but a dog seems to take it right in stride.

AT WORK ALONG U.S. BORDERS · In daily police work, detector dogs must be able to search many different kinds of places: streets, fields, woods, streams, cars, houses, barns, offices, warehouses, airports, railroad stations, bus terminals, small boats, and big ships.

Large airports, seaports, and border points on highways and railroads often use detector dogs trained not by the police but by other government agencies. Since 1970 many narcotics-detector dogs have been trained by the U.S. Customs Service at Front Royal, Virginia, to search for illegal drugs coming into the United States from other countries.

Each Customs narcotics officer works with two dogs. That way, neither dog tires in the long days of constant searching of luggage, freight, mail, planes, cars, buses, trucks, trains—whatever comes into the United States. The dogs find drugs in all kinds of strange hiding places, such as stuffed toys, cans of hairspray or deodorant, and candy bars.

Trained detector dogs help the U.S. Customs Service by quickly searching containers of all kinds.

Narcotics-detecting dogs are so speedy and accurate, they can check out four hundred to five hundred packages in about a half hour. A dog can, in fact, check out in five minutes what it would take a person twenty minutes to examine.

In just one year, 218 narcotics dogs working for the U.S. Customs Service detected 60,958 pounds (27,674 kilograms) of marijuana, 14 pounds (6.3 kilograms) of hashish, 13,165 pounds (5,976 kilograms) of cocaine, 204 pounds (92 kilograms) of heroin, 38 pounds (17 kilograms) of hash oil, 76 pounds (34 kilograms) of opium, 8 pounds (3.6 kilograms) of morphine, 2,648,849 dangerous drugs in the form of pills and capsules. They also found $39,667,495 in drug-tainted cash. All together, the value of the cash and drugs came to almost $816 million.

Drugs are not the only thing United States authorities try to keep from being carried illegally into the country. The U.S. Department of Agriculture trains dogs to detect fruits, vegetables, meats, plants, animals, and plant and animal products. Some of these can carry insects or diseases that could harm U.S. plants and animals.

In the 1920s, for instance, foot-and-mouth disease came to this country in some sausage. Many cattle, sheep, hogs, and other hoofed animals were infected, and the American livestock business was almost ruined before the disease was brought under control.

In 1930 a beetle arrived from Europe carrying a fungus that wiped out half the American elms in the United States. And an orange in somebody's luggage is suspected of bringing the Mediterranean fruit fly into the United States in 1980. The "medflies" multiplied fast and were soon devouring fruits and vegetables in many California gardens. It cost about $100 million to wipe them out.

A USDA dog on the job at those times could have saved everyone a great deal of money and trouble!

A variety of breeds of dogs (all skilled in retrieving) do customs work, and most of them come from animal shelters. Labrador, golden, and other retrievers are most often used. Other breeds include Brittany spaniels, German shorthaired pointers, and, once in a while, a weimaraner, a Doberman pinscher, or a German shepherd.

Beagles, for many years a favorite dog of rabbit and fox hunters, are also a great favorite with the U.S. Department of Agriculture. Troops of these dogs and handlers, called "Beagle Brigades," work with USDA officials in international airports in New York, San Francisco, and other big cities all over the United States. Every day, each brigade makes between twenty and sixty "hits" on illegal material.

Besides its keen nose, a beagle's small size and winsome, puppylike looks make it an ideal detector dog for searching airports. Beagles can get into crowded spaces among suitcases. They can also roam through airport terminals—sniffing luggage, tote bags, packages, and purses—without scaring people who might be afraid of larger, more powerful-looking dogs.

A USDA beagle "hits" on a contraband banana.

When a beagle "hits" on food, plant, or animal, it sits down next to the suitcase, package, or person where it detects the scent. The dog's USDA partner takes over the search. Cookies, nuts, and coffee are legal, and after being checked are allowed to go on their way through customs. But foods such as meat, oranges, lemons, and limes are illegal—and are not permitted into the country. Illegal foods have been found hidden in shoes, coats, belts, even in such innocent-looking things as baby strollers.

Thousands of illegal plants, animals, and their products are detected each year by officers and dogs on duty at points of entry into the United States.

WONDERFUL NOSES · There is hardly anything that a good detector dog cannot be trained to search for.

In England, France, Italy, and other European countries, dogs are taught to hunt for truffles. A truffle is a dark-colored fungus that grows pea size, walnut size, even orange size. Truffles are used on certain foods, such as omelets and salads, to make them tastier (the way mushrooms, for instance, are used on top of pizzas).

Truffles grow wild in bunches around the roots of trees such as oaks and beeches. Pigs are good at finding truffles, but many truffle gatherers have found that dogs are even better. When dogs find truffles they sit down and bark for their partners to come and dig. Pigs, on the other hand, start digging on their own and often gobble up the truffles before their partners catch up to them. Dogs can sniff truffles under ice or snow; pigs cannot. Dogs are much easier to train than pigs, and they do not tire as quickly. It is no wonder that truffle dogs are so often preferred to pigs.

Some businesses train dogs as detectives. One lumber company in Sweden uses dogs to sniff out mold on lumber, since

This dog's keen nose has helped it find a rare truffle, prized by gourmets.

mold often destroys wood. A gas company trains dogs to detect gas leaks. A pest-control company uses a beagle to sniff out termites and carpenter ants that destroy buildings.

More and more uses are being found all the time for dogs' terrific sniffing abilities. Who knows where dogs' noses will lead next? Wherever it may be, you may be sure that dogs will have a good time playing the old hide-and-seek game in a new way.

FURTHER READING

Cole, Joanna. *A Dog's Body*. New York: Morrow, 1986.

Curtis, Patricia. *Dogs on the Case*. New York: Dutton, 1989.

Davidson, Margaret. 7 *True Dog Stories*. Mamaroneck, N.Y.: Hastings House, 1977.

Fichter, George S. *Working Dogs*. New York: Watts, 1979.

Kern, Francis. *German Shepherds*. Hauppauge, N.Y.: Barron's, 1985.

Lauber, Patricia. *The Story of Dogs*. New York: Random House, 1966.

McCloy, James. *Dogs at Work*. New York: Crown, 1979.

Walsh, James E. *Golden Retrievers*. Neptune, N.J.: TFH Publications, 1980.

INDEX

ABOUT THE AUTHOR

Free-lance writer and editor Elizabeth Ring is a former teacher and an editor at *Ranger Rick's Nature Magazine*. Her previous books for children include two biographies, *Rachel Carson: Caring for the Earth* and *Henry David Thoreau: In Step With Nature*, published by The Millbrook Press. She has also written a range of programs on environmental subjects for the National Wildlife Federation. She lives in Woodbury, Connecticut, with her husband, writer and photographer William Hennefrund. Although five dogs have been a part of the family over the years, three cats are their current companions.